WHAT TO DO WHEN GOD SHOWS UP

A STORY OF HEALING

Teresa Aeschliman

Illustrations inspired
by the artwork of
Barbara Johnson

With so much love to
Troy, Ethan, and Ayden.
This book would not exist
without your unwavering
encouragement.

Special thanks to:

Pauline Holsopple, Barbara Johnson, Elaine Moyer, Jay Aeschliman, Deborah Aeschliman, Conrad Holsopple and Tonya Miller for keeping this story alive and continuing to expect and recognize miracles big and little;

Nancy Hastings Sehested, Missy Harris, Rachel Bowman-Abdi, Jil Meadows, Mona Ellum and Ajita Reddy for your story telling and editing talents, and for spurring this project on through the rough patches.

God truly shows up in all of you!

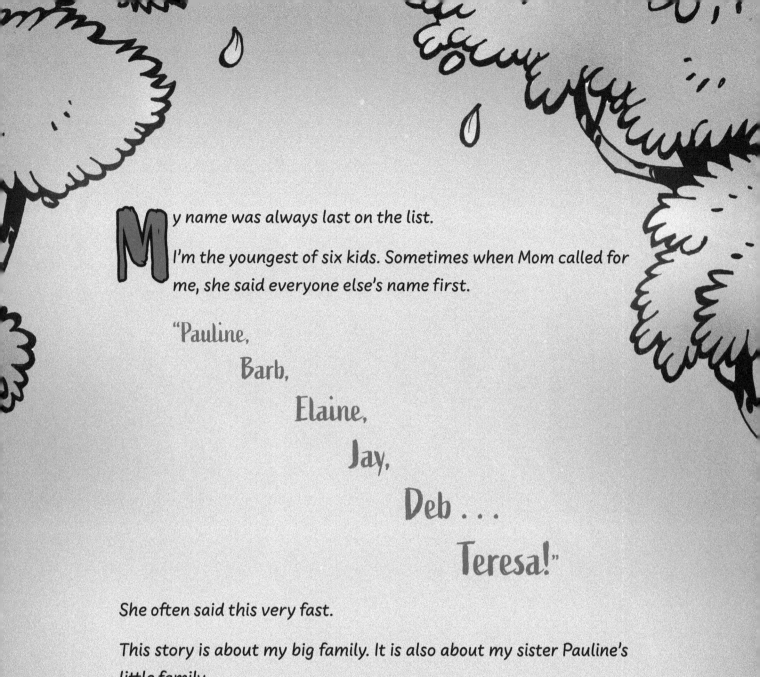

My name was always last on the list.

I'm the youngest of six kids. Sometimes when Mom called for me, she said everyone else's name first.

"Pauline,
        Barb,
                Elaine,
                        Jay,
                                Deb . . .
                                        Teresa!"

She often said this very fast.

This story is about my big family. It is also about my sister Pauline's little family.

My big family lived on a farm in Ohio with cattle, pigs, and chickens. Our dogs, Shag and Champ, kept the barn cats on the run. Our pony, Sugarfoot, didn't like to give rides.

At the time of this story, Pauline, Barb, Elaine, and Jay had grown up and moved away. Deb and I were the only kids living on the farm.

Pauline and her little family lived in Indiana. She had married Paul, and they had two kids: Conrad, who was 5, and Tonya, who was 3.

Conrad and Tonya liked to play in their big yard. Conrad liked to help his dad work on antique cars. Tonya liked to help her mom in their family's bookstore.

One evening, while Mom, Dad, Deb, and I were eating dinner, the telephone rang. Mom answered; it was bad news. Pauline, Conrad, and Tonya had been in a car accident and were all taken to the hospital.

What To Do When You Get Bad News:

Try not to panic.

Say a quick prayer.

"Finish eating your peas!"

Pile the dishes in the sink.

Climb into the green VW bus.

Hold on tight to Chubb the Bear.

Drive for more than an hour to the hospital.

During the crash, Tonya had landed on the floor of the car, near the brake pedal. At the hospital, a doctor put stitches in Tonya's hand. She had lots of bruises. Conrad had lots of bruises, too. They were both sore for many days, but they didn't have to stay in the hospital.

What To Do After a Bad Accident:

Try to keep Tonya from twirling on her tiptoes and tearing her stitches.

Try to keep Conrad from using his bed as a tumbling mat.

Sing a little song.

Say a bedtime prayer.

Tuck them in and hope they stay there!

Pauline had to stay in the hospital. Her jaw was broken in three places, and both of her arms were broken.

Late that night, Dad, Deb, and I bounced home in the green VW bus.
Mom stayed at the hospital to be with Pauline.

What To Do When You're Exhausted from Staying Up Too Late:

Pretend to be asleep so Dad carries you to bed.

Snuggle under the covers with your stuffed animals.

Say a little prayer.

Sing yourself a little song.

Try not to drool on Chubb the Bear because he hates that.

I was still tired when Dad woke me for school the next morning. It seemed like Chubb the Bear had been tromping around on the bed during the night.

What To Do When You Haven't Had Enough Sleep, But You Still Have To Go To Second Grade:

Drag yourself out of bed.

Pull on your favorite sweater-vest.

Try to find matching socks.

Give up on finding matching socks.

Make sure Dad gives you orange juice and not coffee with your cereal.

"Run! You're going to miss the bus!"

After school, Deb and I quickly did our chores, so we could go back to the hospital with Dad.

What To Do When You Get Home from School:

Change into chore clothes.

Go pick up eggs.

Feed the pigs.

Change back into school clothes, because
these are the best smelling option.

Climb into the green VW bus.

Stretch out on the first seat, so Deb has to sit in the back.

Loudly sing all the songs you can think of to keep
Dad awake on the long drive.

Conrad and Tonya would spend a lot of time in the waiting room at the hospital. They weren't allowed to see their mom because she was in the Intensive Care Unit. They were too young to go to that part of the hospital.

What To Do When You Are Bored in the Hospital Waiting Area:

Climb over the furniture.

Climb under the furniture.

Stack the furniture into a tower. Wait! Don't do this.

"Let's color a picture."

"Maybe we should read."

One evening, Dad and Paul went to look at the car Pauline had been driving. Dad told us he felt overwhelmed when he saw the smashed car. "No wonder Pauline was so badly hurt," he said. "I'm shocked Conrad and Tonya only had minor injuries."

Dad said that after seeing the smashed car he walked back to Paul's car and slumped in the back seat to pray. While he was praying, he saw a vision appear before him.

In the vision, everyone in our big family was together, Dad said. It was a scene from Christmas, and Pauline was there, too! All of us were happy and healthy.

Dad said he didn't know if the vision meant our family would all be together again on Earth or in heaven. But what he did know was that God was watching over us and caring for all of us —especially Pauline.

Barb said she wanted to help take care of Pauline's little family, so she left her job teaching art in Chicago and went to live with Conrad, Tonya, and Paul.

What To Do When Kids Miss Their Mom:

Play silly games.

Cook hotdogs.

Sing songs.

Bake cookies.

Help them giggle.

Hold them when they cry.

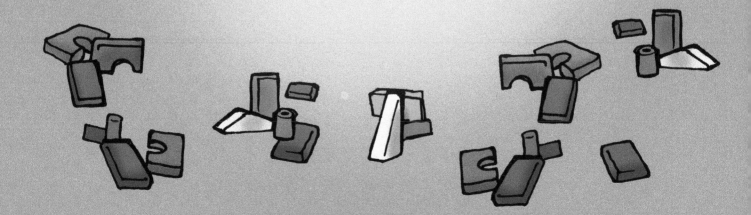

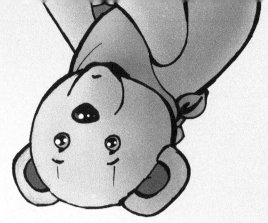

At the hospital, Pauline was getting worse.
The doctors said she needed emergency surgery.

What To Do When Your Sister Is in Surgery:

Quietly sing all the songs you can think of.

Pray.

Hide under the furniture.

Decide to sit on the furniture and hold hands.

After the surgery, doctors told us the inside of Pauline's body looked like a freight train had gone through it. They did their best to repair as much of the damage as they could. But they said that from now on, Pauline would need help from machines to keep her body working. They said she would never be healthy again.

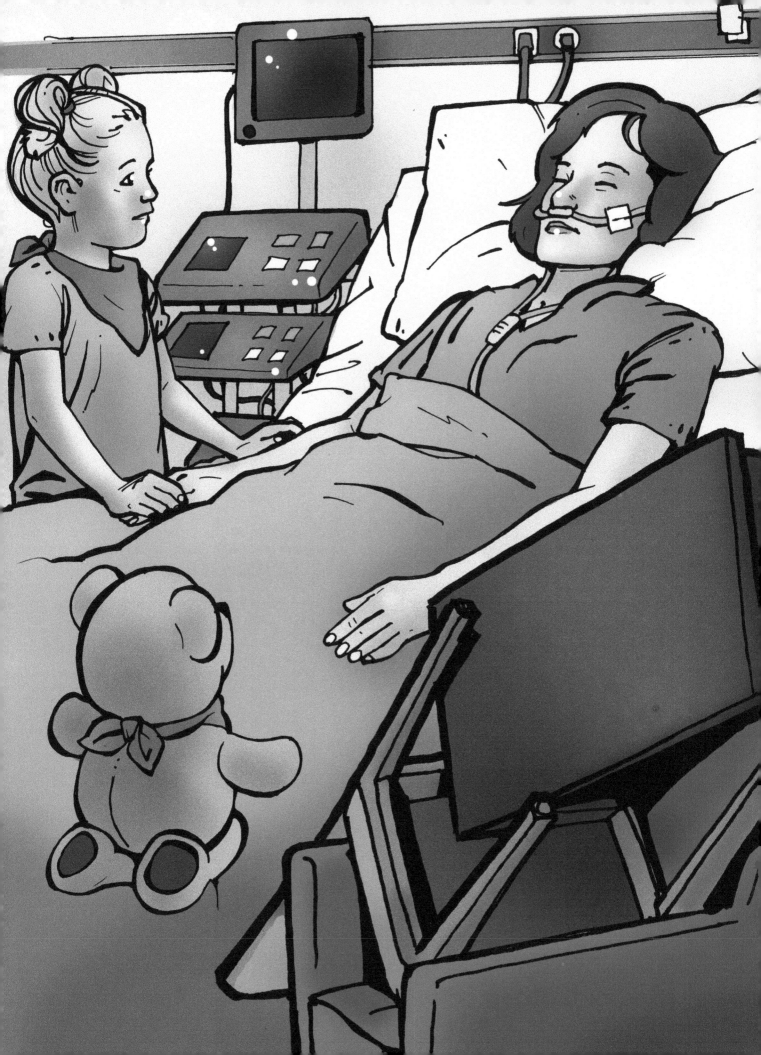

After the surgery, there were a lot of tubes going into and out of Pauline's body: some so she could breathe, some to drain fluids and infection, and some to feed her. She couldn't eat hotdogs.

Pauline was so sick she went into a coma. When someone is in a coma, they look like they are sleeping, but they aren't just asleep. There is no way to wake them.

What To Do When Your Sister Is in a Coma:

Sing her one of her favorite songs.

Tell her a story about a happy time together.

Remind her how fun it is to bake and eat cookies!

Make a furniture tower beside her bed.
Wait! Don't do this.

Give her hand a gentle squeeze
and tell her you love her.

Pauline was not getting better. The doctors said there was nothing more they could do for her. They said Pauline was going to die.

That night, Mom held me close. She told me Pauline was going to go live with Jesus. I felt so sad. I could tell Mom felt sad, too.

What To Do When You Are So Sad:

Hug people closely.

Cry.

Pray.

Tell stories about happy times together.

"Let's sing something."

Elaine came home from teaching at a college in Ohio.

Jay came home from studying to be a pilot at a college in Kansas.

Some people from Paul and Pauline's church visited us at the hospital. They said they were studying the book of James in the Bible. They read the part about anointing someone with oil and praying over them for healing. They thought it would be a good idea to have an anointing service for Pauline.

So, our big family gathered in the chapel at the hospital. We stood in a circle and held hands. We prayed to God about Pauline. We said we would love to have Pauline on Earth with us for a longer time, but we wanted God's will for her.

We knew God wanted Pauline to be free from all the tubes and machines. We knew God wanted Pauline to be free from pain. We knew God loved Pauline even more than we did.

What To Do During the Anointing Service for Your Sister:

Squeeze into the circle of family.

Try to keep your eyes closed.

Look at your shoes instead.

Remember to listen to the prayers.

Decide to look at someone else's shoes.

Try not to think about cookies.

While we were praying, Deb began to dance around the circle. She said, "Why are you all crying? Pauline is going to be fine!"

While we were praying in the chapel, Pastor Leonard and Paul went to Pauline's bedside. They put a drop of oil on her forehead, rested their hands on her shoulders, and prayed. Paul told us that while they were praying, he felt a strange presence fill the room and a sudden movement through Pauline's body.

After the anointing service, we visited Pauline's bedside. Someone saw her eyelids move! Someone saw her mouth twitch! Someone felt her finger jerk!

The doctors couldn't explain what was happening, but Pauline's body showed signs of life.

By the next morning, Pauline wasn't in a coma anymore!

What To Do When You Are So Excited Because Your Sister Is Getting Better:

Hug people closely.

Sing!

Pray!

Climb over the furniture!

Climb under the furniture!

Stack the furnit— wait! No.

"Go play outside!"

As Pauline got stronger, she didn't need the machines and tubes anymore! The doctors and nurses called Pauline their miracle patient. They didn't understand how she was getting better, but we knew God was healing Pauline.

The nurses taking care of Pauline said they heard her singing in a beautiful way they had never heard before. They said it was like listening to an angel sing.

As Pauline was recovering, she shared with us that she had had a vision of dying. She remembered choosing to not stay dead. It was a hard choice.

Pauline told us that, in the vision, she went through a dark tunnel and emerged into a brilliant light. She heard God's voice and felt an overwhelming sense of love.

"I wanted to stay there with God," Pauline said, "but I knew my family needed me. I remember God saying to me, 'Life on Earth will be really hard for a while, but then things will get better.'"

Several weeks before Christmas, Pauline returned home to her little family. Her body was weak and fragile. She wore a wig because her hair had fallen out.

The doctors had warned that Pauline would still need a lot of medical care. But at her next doctor's appointment, the doctor told Pauline she didn't need to come back. Her body was healing, and she would be just fine!

Our big family Christmas on the farm included all of us—even Pauline— just like in Dad's vision!

What To Do When Your Not-Dead Sister Comes To Christmas:

Give her gentle hugs.

Sing Christmas carols.

Tease her about how great her hair looks.

Celebrate new life in baby Jesus and in Pauline!

Eat lots of cookies!

Sometimes God shows up in big ways. Sometimes God shows up in little ways.

God doesn't always heal people like God healed Pauline. Sometimes God heals people in heaven instead of on Earth. The best part of this story is that God always loves us, is always with us, and always wants what is best for us.

What

do you do

when

God

shows

up?

Tell Your Story

When bad things happen, we can feel sad, afraid, or alone. What feelings do you experience when you get bad news?

Talking to God, singing, and taking care of ourselves and others can help us feel better. What do you do to feel better?

Sometimes we forget to look for God. What are some big and little ways you see God?

FriesenPress

One Printers Way
Altona, MB R0G 0B0
Canada

www.friesenpress.com

ISBN
978-1-03-913693-9 (Hardcover)
978-1-03-913692-2 (Paperback)
978-1-03-913694-6 (eBook)

1. *JUVENILE NONFICTION, RELIGIOUS, CHRISTIAN, INSPIRATIONAL*
2. *INSPIRATIONAL AND PERSONAL GROWTH*
3. *SOCIAL TOPICS, EMOTIONS AND FEELINGS*

Distributed to the trade by The Ingram Book Company

About the Author

Teresa Aeschliman details an inspiring story of faith and healing from her childhood in her debut publication, *What To Do When God Shows Up.* Narrating as her seven-year-old self, Teresa tells the story of her sister's car accident and weaves whimsy into the ways in which her family came together in faith. Teresa hopes to inspire children to see that God is in all moments—the joyous, the frustrating, the sad, and the silly.

Teresa grew up in a Mennonite family on a farm near Archbold, Ohio, with a herd of cattle, oodles of pigs, too many chickens, not enough dogs, scary barn cats and an obstinate pony. Even though there were plenty of chores, there was always time for a bit of silliness.

She lives on a mountain near Asheville, North Carolina, with her husband, Troy, and their sons, Ethan and Ayden. Her "What-To-Do" lists these days include early morning hikes, green tea, and dark chocolate.

To learn more about this story,
find resources to help kids tell their stories, and
contact the author, please visit
NoWordsPress.org

CPSIA information can be obtained
at www.ICGtesting.com
Printed in the USA
LVHW071511101222
734970LV00037B/955